THE
Archive Photographs
SERIES

CENTRAL
MANCHESTER

Parker Street in the fifties, with Mosley Street running across the top of the picture. York Street is to the left of the car park and alongside Parker Street itself the ground is being broken for the Piccadilly Plaza where the old warehouses stood till 1940. There is a fine selection of pre- and post-war British cars. A sign high above York Street exhorts us to "Fly BEA Viscount." The "Halifax" is in Mosley Street, beside Yates the Seedsmen while an enormous "Mothers Pride" loaf is high on the next building. For better or for worse, the city centre of today is starting to take shape. (Photograph courtesy of the Manchester Evening News.)

THE
Archive Photographs
SERIES
CENTRAL
MANCHESTER

Compiled by
Peter Stewart

CHALFORD

The Chalford Publishing Company
St Mary's Mill, Chalford,
Stroud, Gloucestershire, GL6 8NX

ISBN 0 7524 0322 2

Typesetting and origination by
The Chalford Publishing Company
Printed in Great Britain by
Redwood Books, Trowbridge

Ardwick, c.1908. (Detail, see p. 130)

Contents

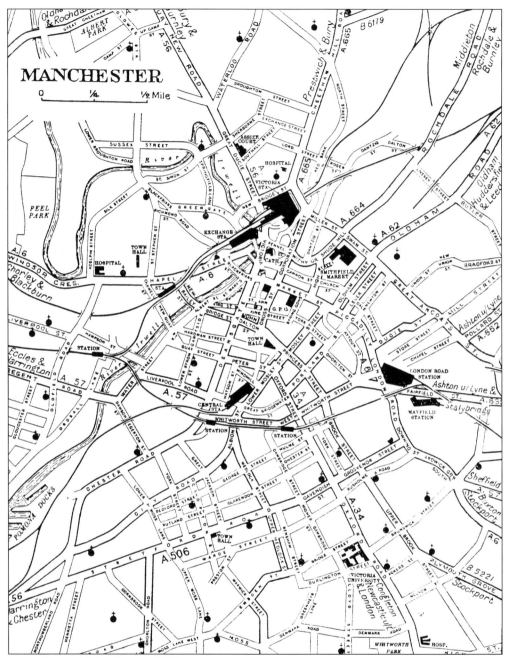

Map of central Manchester, 1930s.

Introduction

Manchester – "Mancunium" the Romans called it, the Victorians "Cottonopolis." Manchester's been called a few things since, not all of them polite, but then which great city hasn't? It has had its ups and downs, like all its peers, but in the last few years its place as the business and cultural capital of the north has been shown to be as secure as ever. It is plain that Manchester intends to be one of the great European cities of the twenty-first century.

Described before the industrial revolution as "the largest . . . village in England," its population rose from about 200,000 in the eighteen forties to three quarters of a million less than a hundred years later. The city entered the twentieth century with enormous confidence, splendid public buildings in the approved, exuberant Victorian style, a slum problem as bad as, but probably no worse than, other towns' and a brand new Ship Canal. If "muck meant brass" the air the citizens breathed was testimony to Manchester's wealth.

The city's past has been as distinguished as it has at times been turbulent. This collection of photographs is a record of the city in the twentieth century, up to, but stopping short of, such things as urban motorways, shopping malls and supertrams. Not pretending to be a full history of the times it is, though, meant to be rather more than an anecdotal snapshot album. Very many of the pictures are from a collection of postcards, a medium the popularity of which began with the new century, but photographs from other sources have been used too and thanks are due to the people who have made this possible and who have been exceptionally helpful in providing background information. The book deals with the city centre and "inner-city" districts, but not the outer suburbs.

The nineteenth century was a time of transformation, but for the next forty years change in the face, if not in the life, of the city was gradual. A few old landmarks went, such as the Royal Infirmary and St Peter's Church and some worthy new business houses were built, but nothing very adventurous was seen, except perhaps the two "skyscrapers" of Deansgate. Near the end of the period, though, the two great new civic buildings beside the Town Hall appeared. Then two long nights just before Christmas 1940 saw the city's face changed for ever with the Shambles disappearing, many fine buildings blasted or burnt beyond repair and 30,000 homes destroyed or damaged with much loss of life. The official "City of Manchester Plan 1945" would, in time, have cleared away much that the Luftwaffe left, but, although some photographs show scenes unrecognisable today, the basic street plan of the city centre remains much as it was. Most major redevelopment, anyway, has taken place fairly recently and is outside the scope of this book.

A city is more than its streets and buildings. Pictures of people at work, at play or just going about, give life to a scene and chart the sociological changes in such things as dress, recreation and transport. Progress and change being inevitable and needed, it is not enough simply to indulge a sentimental nostalgia for times when most were materially worse off. It seems useful, though, to remind ourselves of what was (and many can recall something of those days) and, for those who know today's city, to judge how well Manchester has adapted to the new demands of the last hundred years or so and how well it is succeeding in being a city good to live in, good to work in and good to visit.

The city is too big and varied to give a full portrait of half a century and more of its life in these pages. There are omissions though not, it is to be hoped, too many errors. Pictures have been chosen for their interest and relevance more than for artistic merit, though a few may not lack that too. Rather than arrange them chronologically, it seems more useful to group them by street and area, though the route may be a little tortuous. This work is a record, not a critique. Even if we admit though, that perfection in a city remains a Utopian dream, we can join with that old rhymster Richard Baines in chanting his refrain:

"Sing Ned, sing Joe, sing Fred so gaily,
Manchester's improving daily."

Surely as true now as it was in 1844.

One

Piccadilly and Market Street

Piccadilly has long been at the centre of the city. Queen Victoria still sits here on her throne, with the gardens behind and the hustle and bustle before her. The great open space of Piccadilly Gardens has survived since 1908 when the Infirmary moved away. It has always been a busy place, a starting point for journeys to almost anywhere around. Piccadilly Station decants its passengers into the top of the street and the lower end leads straight into Market Street, its stores and shops and, now, the huge Arndale Centre. It has seen an Art Gallery planned but, like last century's replacement Cathedral, never built, a cinema and the B.B.C. come and go. Trams from half a dozen concerns used to mingle here. While all the horses have trotted off, the evolving history of the motor vehicle has been paraded in their stead. And still, a returning Edwardian would know the place. Market Street grew from the medieval Market Stead Lane to become the place to shop, more cheap and cheerful than King Street or the long stretch of Deansgate. It was a vital route to and from Piccadilly, now a function of Cannon Street. Bonnie Prince Charlie lodged here in 1745 and Queen Victoria came up in style in 1851. They would scarcely recognise it now, pedestrianised beyond High Street and plunging under cover on its way towards Deansgate.

Inter-City travellers, and many passengers by air, now first set foot in Manchester from Piccadilly Station in London Road (and known by that name until the early sixties, when it was reconstructed.) The close-up view shows the London & North Western named with the Manchester, Sheffield and Grimsby Railway, with a long list of destinations. This handsome building was opened in 1842, but the whole facade has now been replaced. The view of London Road and the station approach, with its long line of cabs, is full of period detail (see facing page). The Grotto Cafes in Stevenson Square offer 4-course meals for one shilling (5p.) and *The Return of the Prodigal* is on at the Gaiety. (PPCs: Artistic Series 1; Kingsway, S2251, c.1910.)

Whitworth Street meets London Road just past the railway station and the new Fire Station, faced in terra cotta, was built in 1902, the building also housing the Coroner's Court. The tram is coming down Whitworth Street, to cross London Road into Fairfield Street. The building survives, though not as a fire station. (PPC, Chas. Wilkinson 95, c.1904.)

QUEENS HOTEL. MANCHESTER.

The Queen's Hotel, at the corner of Piccadilly and Portland Street, long had a reputation as the most luxurious in the city, with the finest cuisine. The building dated form 1852. A modern hotel now stands on the site. (PPC, Blum & Degen, c.1900.)

Technical School, Manchester

The Technical School, later the College of Technology, had earned world-wide fame and prestige long before becoming UMIST. The main entrance, in Sackville Street, is on the right of the picture, which is taken across Whitworth Street. The building, described as being of terra cotta and Accrington brick (said to be the hardest building brick there is) with a roof of Tilberthwaite green slate, has lasted from the start of the century and is incorporated into the new Institute. (PPC, Valentine 69187, c.1911.)

Demolished in 1908, the Royal Infirmary had been here since 1755. The bird's-eye view shows the old building in its final shape. The Portland Street and Parker Street warehouses form the backdrop and the prominent tower of the Police Courts in Minshull Street looms behind. During the demolition the Accident Room in Parker Street remains open, the posters tell. (PPCs: Grosvenor, 1907; A.H. & S.M.)

Piccadilly in the 1930's. A solitary 19 tram, completing its journey from Hyde, moves past the site of the old Infirmary on its way to the Exchange terminus. The Duke of Wellington broods over the scene, for once almost traffic-free. (PPC, John Rodgers & Sons (Chapelmoor) Ltd., 206-6.)

Piccadilly, Manchester.

1909

Post-war Piccadilly. Not a lot has changed by the forties. The Gardens remain a peaceful oasis. Buses are replacing the old trams, which clank off for good in January 1949. The Rylands building was built in the twenties. As well as its projecting clock it has a beacon on the roof "as an aid to aviators." The statue at the Mosley Street corner is of Robert Peel, erected, like the Duke's, in 1856. (PPCs: J.Salmon Ltd., 19098, c.1949; Valentine H5321, 1948.)

PICCADILLY, MANCHESTER.

HS321

The Gardens, about 1930. The gardener is busy tending a fine show of blooms. The symbolic sculpture is called "Adrift." The Parker Street warehouses bear some historic names: J. Templeton & Co., Staines Inlaid Linoleum, Peel, Watson & Co.

Parker Street on 23 December 1940. The conflagration extended round into Portland Street and could only be controlled by dynamiting unaffected buildings in its path. This blaze which destroyed the line of warehouses was said to be the biggest fire in Britain since 1666, a doubtful honour which was lost one week later when London suffered its greatest fire bomb raid.

Oldham Street is seen to be a busy shopping street in Edwardian days, though its character changes as it goes towards New Cross and Oldham Road. James Lowe's store, foreground, sports an eagle over the entrance. Opposite, Yates's Wine Lodge is an old-established favourite. By the thirties, though, Lowe and his eagle have flown and C. & A.'s modern store looks across to Yates's where a three-course lunch (of a sort) can still be had for 6d. ($2\frac{1}{2}$ p.). Beyond C. & A.'s is Lomas's, while Woolworth's, where nothing is ever more than sixpence, advertises "Special Values – Sale This Week." Beat that! (PPCs: Valentine, c.1903; Valentine 216357, 1932.)

Parker Street has been an open bus station for most of the century. Lewis's store, in Mosley Street, but with its main front round the corner in Market Street, is still there today but Wiles' wonderful toy shop is only a fond memory, for some of us, of the days when we were young. The Piccadilly Cinema was once where Littlewood's store is seen. The Rylands building at the top of Market Street is now Debenham's and Woolworth's, at the corner of Oldham Street, is among many no longer here. The Gardens look as well-cared for as ever, and well used. (Photographs courtesy of the *Manchester Evening News*.)

Lewis's has dominated the top of Market Street as long as most people can remember. The advertising card, posing as a "real photograph" has, allowing for artistic licence, some relation to reality, for it is a big building indeed. The covered opening between the store and Wiles' was a useful rendezvous where it was possible to shelter from the rain while waiting. It is now blocked off by a new shop.

It is early thirties now, looking up the street, with Rylands building top left. New Brown Street is in the left foreground and half-way up on the right is Spring Gardens, leading to the General Post Office. (PPC, Valentine 216361, 1932.)

The High Street corner, where Hope Bros. faced Horne Bros. Boots' and H.Samuel are further down and then a giant poster tells of a big stock clearance. On the other side, Barratt (shoes) has a Duncan & Foster van outside and The Don (tailors) beyond. It is the mid-twenties. The 47 tram is on its way to Altrincham, a service which survived rail electrification by four weeks in 1931. Things have gone full circle, with trams now running on those railway tracks. (PPC, Valentine 98528, 1926.)

The General Post Office, often said to be the second most important in the kingdom, and built in the Italian Renaissance style in Spring Gardens, backing on to Brown Street, is no longer. There is a Post Office here, but it is hard to describe its architectural style. (PPC, Valentine, c.1914.)

The tram track curves into Shude Hill from the far end of High Street by way of Nicholas Croft with Withy Grove opening on the left. Back Turner Street runs off to the right. The depression is here and bargains are on offer: "Gramophones Below Cost" and a "Revolution in Prices" at the opticians, "Shell Wear (tortoiseshell?) including Sight Testing, 5/- (25p.)" Hospital Sunday, for the annual appeal, advertised on the tram standard, was February 9th. (Photograph courtesy of City Engineer, February 1930.)

The Clarion Cafe at 50a Market Street, with its decorative entrance and high-backed chairs in the Oak Room looks to be in the style prevalent in many another tea-room or cafe at the turn of the century, when they flourished as a place where "respectable" ladies out shopping could take a non-alcoholic refreshment in congenial company and surroundings. The name "Clarion" though declares its Socialist origins, part of the nationwide movement which stemmed from the founding of Robert Blatchford's "Clarion" newspaper in 1894. Decoration included eight panels by Bernard Sleigh illustrating "The King's Lesson" by William Morris. Opened in 1903, it closed in 1936 to become a rather classy Kardomah cafe, fitted out in gently curving panels of wood in warm, restful shades featuring small back-lit insets concerned with tea and coffee. The "Clarion Cafe" at the Pump House Galleries commemorates the name, without attempting to be a replica. (PPCs published by Clarion Cafe.)

Clarion Cafe Entrance.
50a Market St., Manchester

Manchester Clarion Café—
Oak Room.

The Royal Exchange tower is seen in the distance. Brown Street is on the left and opposite, at New Brown Street, Redfern's advertise their "Razors, Safety Razors and Blades." "Onoto, All British Pens" and "The Reston Waltham Watch, Plumb on the Second" are prominently named on the buildings. Shops include A. & S. Walker, with lots of framed pictures, Dolcis shoes and Withecombe's. The Clarion Cafe is half-way down on the left. (PPC, Valentine, 86526, 1922.)

Where Market Street meets Cross Street and Corporation Street, one of the busiest spots in the city. Here, in the mid-twenties, a 29 tram bound for Trafford Park keeps company with a Slack & Cox mineral water lorry and a mix of private cars including three open roadsters. (PPC, Valentine, 98538, 1926.)

MARKET STREET, MANCHESTER.   C.600.

The entire length of Market Street is seen here. Beaty Bros., the outfitters at the corner of Victoria Street, are not to be confused with Batty the jeweller, whose clock shows a quarter past five on a mid-thirties afternoon. The Royal Exchange casts its shadow on the right. The three brass balls of Prosser the pawn can just be seen on the extreme left. (PPC, Valentine, G600, 1934.)

Two

Cross Street and St Anne's Square

The first part of Cross Street is dominated by the Royal Exchange building, and the opposite side was once the home of the Manchester Guardian and its sister Evening News. Further along and opposite St Ann Street, the plain, Georgian, Cross Street Chapel stood until December 1940. The rest of the street has traditionally been for business, rather than shopping, though Boots' the Chemists and "Fags," the little barber shop in the Exchange building will be remembered by many, as will Sherratt & Hughes' bookshop. The greatest change in Cross Street in recent years has been the coming of the great wall of the Arndale Centre, facing the Exchange and bridging Market Street. St Anne's Square, with St Ann's Church (the final "e" seemed to attach only to the Square and has now been dropped altogether) at one end, and the short Exchange Street at the other, is a Georgian creation among whose first occupants were the Jacobite army in 1745. St Ann's was built in 1712 , originally with a three-tier spire. At the other end of the square the massive Exchange building extends right along Exchange Street. The building was severely damaged in the blitz and the opposite side of the street disappeared entirely.

An Edwardian view towards Market Street shows the *Guardian* office opposite the Exchange with the name of the rival "Courier" also prominent. Beyond, another vertical sign names J.S. Moss & Sons, tailors. The "S" stood for Slazenger and Mr Moss later moved to London and founded the sports goods firm. (PPC, Rapid Photo Co., V266-5, 1906.)

The Cross Street front of the Royal Exchange, as altered in 1870, boasted a fine colonnade and much embellishment, but to gain space this was replaced in 1921 to give a convex face to the street. (PPC, Valentine 46582, 1905.)

The New Royal Exchange after the frontage was pushed out into Cross Street, making the trading floor the largest uninterrupted one anywhere. The shops in the basement included Boots' the Chemists' main Manchester store. The building is now the home of the Royal Exchange Theatre; the trading floor is gone, and so has Boots. (PPC, JLB.)

A corner of the floor. Its magnificence is clearly seen. The boards indicate that it is 14 June, and there is evidence in the backgound that the workmen doing the alterations have not quite finished. (PPC, Valentine 86247, 1922.)

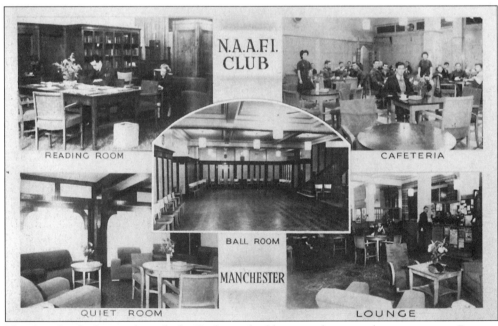

The Arcade which runs through the Exchange building now houses a shopping centre. Pre-war it was a dark tunnel with the Manchester Limited Restaurant on one side and the Cafe on the other. These became the N.A.A.F.I. Club for the forces and remained so for a few years after the war. (PPC, Photocrom Co., London, 1940's.)

The *Manchester Evening News* survives and thrives in Deansgate, as the city's one remaining evening paper. A vignette on a novelty postcard shows the entrance to the Advertising Department behind the front page of 17 May 1904. One classified ad. offers a "LARGE CORNER WINDOW TO LET, with a splendid view of the Whit processions." A bill on the pavement tells of Test Match news.

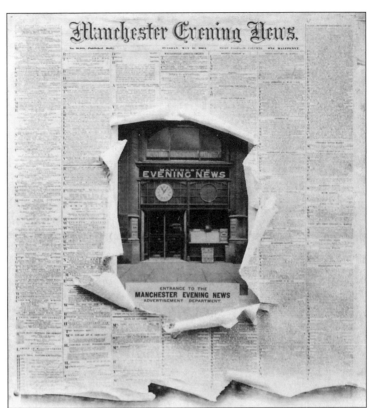

Cross Street in the mid-seventies and the Arndale Centre, near completion, stretching away into the distance as far as Cannon Street, has replaced the old *Guardian* and *Evening News* home as well as much else. Since this photograph was taken the start of Corporation Street has been bridged to connect the Centre with Marks and Spencer's.

CROSS STREET AND EXCHANGE, MANCHESTER.

Looking back towards Corporation Street in the early twenties, the full length of the Exchange is seen. On a sunny morning the 14 tram is heading for Heaton Park, passing a heavy-laden one-horse wagon, man and boy leading, two more on top. A motor van, passing Percy's tailor shop, implores us to "Eat Almond's Bread." Peter Dawson's Scotch is advertised on a roof-top above the tram. (PPC, Valentine 98552, 1926.)

Opposite: King Street's top half is for business, while that below Cross Street is for retailing, though traditionally not for the economy class shopper. In a view from the top, in the mid-forties, the Manchester Assurance Company office is at No. 98, with the stately headquarters of the Manchester Ship Canal Company next. Lower down on that side is the Bank of England. London Assurance and Vulcan Boiler share premises on the right and at the Cross Street corner is the rusticated frontage of Lloyd's Bank. Before Lloyd's, the 1819 Town Hall had been there. It became the Reference Library after the new Town Hall was built in 1868 and it was taken down in 1911. The portico, though, was saved and still stands in Heaton Park. Back at the top of the street, on the left, a sign points to the nearest Air Raid Shelter, a reminder of the times.. (PPC, Richter, 61686.)

34

The Cross Street Chapel, seen here in the 1920's, was founded in 1694 after the passing of the Act of Toleration, allowing Henry Newcombe, one of the Collegiate Church clergy who had left the established church, to resume preaching in the year before his death. The original building was badly damaged in the Jacobite rising of 1715 and the rebuilt one lasted from 1734 until December 1940 when it was reduced to a shell. The present Chapel, put up in 1958, is in the style of those times and closed temporarily in 1995 for further re-building.

The Bank of England was in King Street from 1845 until 1971 but its dignified home remains here as a solid reminder of its presence. This photograph was taken in the early twenties.

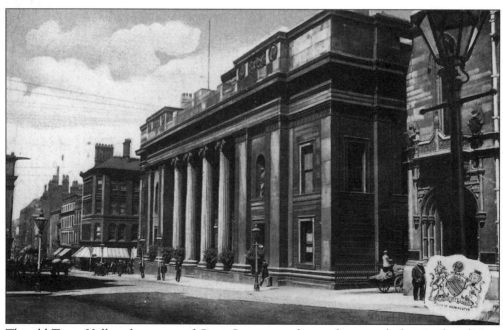

The old Town Hall at the corner of Cross Street, seen here a few years before its demolition. (PPC, "Milton Series," 1908.)

The lower half of King Street in the twenties, looking down to Deansgate. This part has been pedestrianised but otherwise remains as it was, a place for shopping and small offices.

St Ann Street seen in the twenties with the William Deacon's Bank (now part of the Royal Bank of Scotland) building on the opposite side to the church, near the Deansgate end. The bowler hat was practically a badge of office for the businessman then and for many more years.

Past King Street, Cross Street continues to Albert Square. In an Edwardian photograph South King Street is seen opening on the left; the Eagle Insurance Company's handsome building, with its fine wrought-iron balustrade, looks just as good today, ironwork and all. Smith's Pianos are sold on the ground floor. The St Ann Street corner is in the distance on the left and the Reference Library is just visible on the right. The tram, No.138, is one of the city's first batch of electric cars, on the first electrified route, to Hightown. (PPC, Grosvenor, 4, 1911.)

Saint Ann's Square, 1746. (A print from "Berry & Cassons Plan, 1746," reproduced in "Memorials of Manchester Streets," R.W. Procter, pub. Thomas Sutcliffe, Manchester, 1874.)

216569.

CROSS STREET, MANCHESTER.

Looking from Albert Square, in the late thirties, Lloyd's Bank stands on the King Street corner. The first opening on the right is the narrow Tib Lane. There are "HOLIDAY BARGAINS" at Henry's Summer Sale. The Mecca Cafe is in the next building. There are shipping offices on the left, the Union Castle, White Star and Royal Mail lines. The 42 tram, bound for West Didsbury, sports a primitive trafficator, of a design which was not successful as the ends kept being broken off. The building in the left foreground, which turns the corner into John Dalton Street, is said to be on the site of the de Quincey home, where Thomas was born, although his tombstone in Edinburgh names Greenheys. (PPC, Valentine 216569, 1932.)

St Ann's Church is one of the small number of pre-Victorian buildings to survive and continue in its original use. (PPCs, AHC 1715, 2840, mid thirties.)

St Anne's Square in an Edwardian photograph. An enormous placard in front of the church tells of "Mack Hamilton's Lace Curtain Week," starting on May Day. (PPC, WHS S2549.)

Looking towards Exchange Street around 1908. A fine array of hansom cabs awaits custom while businessmen and a few ladies stand around on the pavement or wander onto the roadway. Richard Cobden, in the middle, has his back to us. (PPC, Kingsway 14085.)

Fifty years on, and taxis have replaced the hansoms, while Cobden, the great Free Trader, surveys the uncompromising architecture of post-war Britain. The South African War Memorial is beyond him. Fifties cars and fifties fashions, in the period between the New Look and the Mini-Skirt, fill the Square. Kardomah, on the extreme left, has a crowd outside, but, sadly, Sissons, next door, is To Let. A favourite rendezvous between the wars, a tea-room whose cakes and chocolates could not be beaten, they had a smaller branch across the Square. (PPC, Lilywhite Ltd., Brighouse MHR5.)

Three

Victoria Street and Corporation Street

Victoria Street, which runs all the way from the lower end of Market Street to the railway bridge over the Irwell, was an uninspiring sort of place in its first part, even before the destruction of the massive and gloomy Victoria Buildings in 1940. The remainder of the street was a great open space, graced by the Cathedral and Chetham's Hospital on one side and Exchange Station, across the river, on the other. For several years after the war the triangular Victoria Buildings bomb-site, cleared and laid out as a garden, gave pleasing vistas to show off the Royal Exchange and the Cathedral. Corporation Street was built in the middle of the last century to give a straight route from the city centre to the start of Cheetham Hill Road (York Street, then) and the north. On its lower side the Shambles was then left untouched, a warren of narrow streets and lanes, housing small businesses and provision merchants, centred on the old Market Place. Ancient Long Millgate coursed down to the Cathedral and beside it Victoria Station had been there since 1844. On the other side of Corporation Street another old street, Withy Grove climbed up to Shude Hill.

Victoria Street, seen from Exchange Street with Market Street on the right and St Mary's Gate on the left. The Victoria Buildings occupied the entire left side as far as the junction with Deansgate. Walmsley & Sons (umbrella makers) are seen, with their entrance flanked by a pair of magnificent columns, topped by mythical figures. (PPC, Grenville, c.1905.)

VICTORIA STREET, MANCHESTER.

G.603.

Victoria Buildings, put up in 1878, was built and owned by the Corporation. There was an arcade on the ground floor of the Victoria Buildings but by the thirties this was dark and silent, though one could still wander through. The Victoria Hotel, fortunately, had few guests, one of whom was Dr Garfield Williams, Dean of Manchester, when, on 22 December 1940, incendiaries hit it. He later watched anxiously from a safer place as the Cathedral survived amongst the surrounding inferno, until the very end of the raid when it was hit by a high explosive bomb. (PPC, Valentine G 603, 1934.)

Nothing was left standing in St Mary's Gate. Viewed from the station approach, Woolworth's is seen to have been rebuilt but Parker's restaurant, with its short-lived Art Deco buttery, is only a cherished memory. The half-timbered Wellington Inn and Sinclair's Oyster Bar are about all that is left of the Shambles. (PPC, courtesy of Manchester City Council, 1950's.)

Market Place, the centre of the Shambles, just after the war, with three pre-war cars, including two small Morrises, parked. (PPC, Richter, 61678.)

Another post-war photograph shows the uninterrupted view of the Cathedral which was then possible. The Deansgate Hotel was also bombed and here the upper floors are still a ruin, but Millett's are using the ground floor. The Grosvenor Hotel, at the corner of Victoria Bridge Street, though, is open and busy. Beyond the station approach the road goes under the bridge to Great Ducie Street and Strangeways. (PPC, Valentine K6073, 1953.)

Oliver Cromwell, sword in hand, is seen gazing up Victoria Street in the afternoon sunshine one day in the mid-forties. Legend has it that Queen Victoria, entering the city from Salford, where she had spent the night, was not amused to find the regicide with his back to her. The clutter of trams behind him made it hard to get a good view of the Cathedral, until they were scrapped. Oliver Cromwell had to go too, for he also was reckoned to be in the way of progress. The trams were accorded a funeral pyre behind Hyde Road Depot but Nollie was transported to distant Wythenshawe in 1968. Cavalier treatment indeed. (PPC, Richter 66159, c.1946.)

A view from Victoria buildings . It is midday and trams make up most of the traffic. The river, out of sight below the station approach, is still dark and smelly, awaiting pollution control and a good clean-up. "Guiness is Good for You" reads the poster, the classic slogan that must have been as good for Guiness as Guiness was claimed to be for you. (PPC, Valentine 21653, 1932.)

The tower and south-west aspect of the Cathedral are seen on a view from the thirties. The Cathedral dates from 1422. It was the Collegiate Church (known locally as "th' owd church") until last century, when it was given its new status. There was much restoration and new building in the years 1862-68 and then in 1940 it was so severely damaged that there was at first some doubt whether it could be repaired. Chetham's Hospital is beyond, across Fennel Street. "Farola," a semolina pudding and the northern delicacy, tripe, are advertised on the hoardings. (PPC, Grosvenor 3; AHC 1680.)

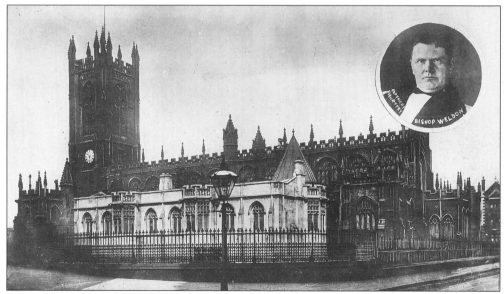

The Cathedral from the south-west, with Bishop Weldon inset. Previously Dean, he was the Bishop from 1906 to 1918. The Victorian addition to the building on its southern aspect has not yet acquired its black coating; further changes have since altered the appearance of this corner. (PPC, Grosvenor 3, Edwardian.)

Exchange Station was actually in Salford, but was reached from Manchester, either by way of the Approach or over the long platform ("the longest in the world") which connected it to Victoria. Opened in 1884, it closed in 1969, to become a car park. The Italianate frontage was destroyed in the blitz and never restored. Cromwell is pictured full face; the base of his statue was a favourite place for loungers and cabbies in the days when it was still possible to sit there and watch the world go by. (PPC, Grosvenor 23, 1905.)

Exchange Station concourse on a quiet morning during King Edward's reign. (PPC, Rainbow Series".)

The Corn and Produce Exchange, now a retail market for all sorts of objects of desire, in its restored state. The Exchange was on this site, between Hanging Ditch and Fennel Street, from 1836. The present building dates from 1903 and in the picture, taken in Hanging Ditch about 1910, the window cleaner is seen hard at work at Parr's Bank. Winn's Cafe, next door, survived both wars. (PPC, Kingsway S6654.)

From Market Place, Fennel Street runs down towards the Cathedral. The Wellington Inn has two cabs waiting outside and beyond the lane, in 1910, John Hayes, Licensed to Deal in Game, has his place. J.Kelsall , Fishmonger is below the Manchester Central Hiring Company Limited. The latter hired servants. (PPC, Grosvenor 14047.)

An early Edwardian view of the Inn, with Will Chambers' fishing rod and fly business above, shows the lane busy with fish and poultry sellers, while the man on his ladder fixes the lamp. Victoria Buildings closes the view at the end of the lane. Compare this with the view on p.47, forty years later. (PPC, Hunt's Series 315.)

The Shambles about 1912 by which time Hanson the Shirtmaker has replaced John Hayes. Samuel Kenyon is the licensee. By the thirties, this corner was famous for Goulburn's, who sold everything from game to Bury Puddings. (PPC, E.A.Schwerdtfeger & Co., London 0565.)

Poets' Corner, in Long Millgate, a building as old as its dilapidated state suggests. The Sun Inn had long been here, but it lost its licence in the 1870's after gaining some notoriety and the building become famous as Ye Olde Curiosity Shop. At one time it shared its premises with a tuck shop, much favoured by the boys from the Grammar School, on the other side of the street. It was taken down in the early twenties. In the view up the street, which dates from the beginning of the century, Turner's Restaurant can be seen at the corner of Todd Street, with the square towers of the old C.W.S. building in the background. (PPC, Valentine 33430; Kingsway S2543, 1910s.)

Victoria Station, opened in 1844, served the London & North Western and Lancashire & Yorkshire Railways then the L.M.S. from 1923. Victoria and Exchange served all parts except the south, but Inter-City services now leave from Piccadilly. A morning view of the concourse shows a scene little changed until a few years ago. Posters advertise the Brussels Exhibition of 1910 and also offer Walking & Cycling Tours. "Mr Balfour and the Crown" is the top news of the day. The domed building at the far end is the restaurant. (PPC, Kingsway, S6647.)

On Number 12 platform trains go for Blackpool, Belfast and Scotland. The *Manchester Guardian* has "Plans for Today's Flight to Manchester" and news of "Mr Balfour & the Veto." Selfridges and various journals advertise and another billposter reads "Girls, Grave Revelations." (PPC, Kingsway S6662, 1910.)

The Co-operative Wholesale Society still has its headquarters in Corporation Street and these buildings remain, flanked by more modern ones. In the thirties the street was usually lined by a fleet of Armstrong Siddely limousines belonging to the Society. The Metrolink trams now cross on their way to Victoria, coming down Balloon Steet, which is between the two buses. Facing the Co-op buildings there are now uninterrupted views of Victoria Station and Chetham's across the parked cars. In this early post-war view the travel agency is, as now, in the near ground floor of the main building. The No.75 bus is headed for Platt Lane. The Autumn fashions have an early thirties look. (PPCs, courtesy of Co-operative Wholesale Society.)

Kemsley House, at the corner of Corporation Street and Withy Grove, replaced an older building in the early thirties. Of the seven titles named on the frontage, only the *Sunday Times* survives. The *Evening Chronicle* first appeared on 10 May 1897, and survived till well after the second war. The *Daily Dispatch* was a respected local broadsheet which also succumbed to the competition, while the Sunday *Empire News* is yet another name from the past. The building stands, but the presses are silent. Pre-war the *Chronicle* was delivered round the city centre from smart pony traps which could often race through the traffic quicker than the vans which replaced them.

Shude Hill Market, part of the complex between that street and Swan Street and Smithfield market. Apart from the produce in the covered area, street stalls sold pets, live poultry and books. (PPC, Kingsway 337, 1908.)

The Rover's Return, Shudehill,
The Oldest Licensed House in Manchester,
dating from A.D. 1306.

318-A.

Manchester had two very ancient inns, each claiming to be the elder but whereas the "Seven Stars" in Withy Grove was the "oldest licensed house in Great Britain," the "Rover's Return" in Shudehill went one better as the "oldest licensed house in Manchester, dating from A.D. 1306." The postcard view of the "Seven Stars" gives its age around 1910 as 540 years, which takes us back to 1370, making it a mere upstart. Both have gone, but of course the "Rover's Return" is immortalised in " Coronation Street." W. Pearson was the licensee at the " Rovers" when the picture was taken. (PPCs: JLB 318-A; Baur's Series 2132.)

The Mitre Hotel, behind the Cathedral, is not just so venerable, but it is still there and welcoming its guests. Starting life in 1815 as "The Old Chuch Inn," the building looks much the same as it did when Fred Slack of Cathedral Yard published this postcard in King Edward's reign.

Cannon Street, now the route for the traffic displaced from Market Street, bridged over in places and noisy, was, in 1930, a quiet, unassuming sort of place, coming down from High Street and then crossing Corporation Street to provide a terminus for trams and buses. The upper part was all warehouses and wholesalers. The view looking up towards High Street shows plenty of variety in the goods advertised. The little cafe at 53 is under new management, and a three course lunch is only one and three (about 6p.) Number 43 is just off the picture; there was the original of the Cheeryble Brothers' warehouse. Dickens visited Manchester often, on visits to his sister and his friend, Harrison Ainsworth, and there met the Grant brothers, William and David, wool & linen drapers whom he describes in the forward to Nicholas Nickleby as performing "every day (and oftenest by stealth) some munificent and generous deed in that town of which they are the pride and honour." Few streets in the city can have changed in character as much as Cannon Street and few can match it for carbon monoxide and other emissions. (Photograph courtesy of City Engineer.)

Four

Deansgate and Oxford Street

Deansgate, straight as any Roman road is known to be, but named after the Danes, and long enough perhaps to have made a grand and fashionable boulevard, attracted many first-rate shops and business names. Kendal Milne, long Manchester's premier department store, is here. It has, too, the city's most acclaimed Victorian building, the John Rylands library. But its character always changed as it neared Knott Mill, with a railway goods yard and depot taking up the east side after Peter Street and then Deansgate disappeared under a cluster of railway bridges. The far end is livelier now, though, with the Castlefield Centre and museums and Granada studios to be found down Liverpool Road. Much of the railway presence is gone and that, plus clean brickwork, makes everything brighter and airier than ever before. All the streets off the west side lead to the Irwell bridges and Salford, which for long jealously guarded its independence against its once predatory neighbour. Peter Street, the link with Oxford Street and the south, took its name from the old church, and St Peter's Fields, site of the "Peterloo Massacre" is now home to the Free Trade Hall. Oxford Street was always the place for entertainment; theatres, cinemas and dance halls.

St Mary's Gate, leading to Market Street, is on the left and Stewart & Stewart, tailors, are on the Blackfriars Street corner. It is the early twenties and the smart, but already anachronistic, Salford tram is nearing its terminus at Victoria Bridge. "Veno's Lightning Cough Cure," made by a Manchester company, ("if it fails no other medicine will ever succeed") had a ready market in industrial Lancashire where bronchitis was rife. The Veno's name survives to this day. (PPC, Valentine 86255, 1922.)

Opposite: The same site as in the picture opposite, showing the remains of Victoria Buildings, across St Mary's Gate. The rather elegant glass dome had been previously invisible from street level but remained briefly as a new feature of the skyline till the demolition squad got round to it.

CITY WALLS

A BUILDING BREAKS UP—DEANSGATE, MANCHESTER.

At the St Mary's Gate corner, a building collapses at the height of the blitz and is pictured by a brave news photographer who probably never took a more dramatic shot.

Deansgate around 1906. Five trams in line, most belonging to Salford Corporation. They are all very new; electric tram services mushroomed in Edwardian days as they, for the first time, gave the ordinary person public transport to get around at much more than walking pace. The coachman is perhaps waiting for his mistress outside F. J. Batchelor's mantle and jacket showrooms. The arched windows of Hayward's Glass & China shop on the left look not much different today, but the business is no longer locally owned. The building, and shopfront, though, are listed, so should survive. (PPC, Rapid Photo Co, V2663.)

Reached down St Mary's Street, the Parsonage Gardens is a welcome oasis off Deansgate. (PPC, Excel Series 39, 1937.)

The same scene as shown opposite, but by 1932 an impressive car, FW42, is there, in place of the coach. The shop now specialises in Silks and Lancashire Fabrics. Barr's toyshop, next door at Number 49, the only serious rival to Wiles', is soon to close. A more modern Salford tram and much more other traffic. Crossing a busy street could be a problem then, too. In both this and the picture opposite the trams hide the entrance to the elegant Barton Arcade which remains to this day, restored to its former glory. (PPC, Valentine, 216566.)

St Ann Street is on the right and St Mary's Street opposite, with the Midland Bank at the corner. Salford tram, Number 166, bound for the Docks, is passing Goodson's. An intriguing notice, in front of the Midland Bank entrance, advertises "Turkish & Russian Baths, Sunday Night." The Cathedral is visible in the distance. (PPC, Valentine, 98522, 1926.)

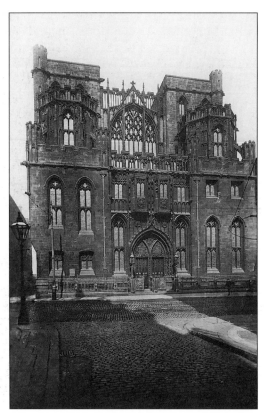

Rylands Library, built between 1890 and 1899 by his widow as a memorial to John Rylands, one of Manchester's foremost merchants, remains untouched, except for cleaning. It houses rare books and manuscripts and is now part of the University of Manchester. (PPC, Kingsway S2554.)

Kendal Milne, now a House of Fraser store, has been in Deansgate since the earlier years of the last century. Originally across the road, it extended to the west side later and built a store which in the thirties was the last word in modernity. (Advertising card, Edwardian.)

DEANSGATE, MANCHESTER.

21665

Northcliffe House, built as the *Daily Mail* offices, has been empty recently, unlike the other "skyscraper" nearby in Atkinson Street, Sunlight House, which surpasses it in height. The Number 54 tram is heading for Seymour Grove from Hightown on a day in the early thirties. Finnigans's, famed for leather goods, advertises vertically in the mid-distance. (PPC, Valentine 216657, 1932.)

The City Hall is, happily, retained as one part of the Museum of Science & Industry, while its twin, higher up Liverpool Road is now the Air & Space Gallery. It was long the city's main exhibition site. The Doll Show in 1912 was in aid of the Cinderella Fund.

WATER STREET RAILWAY BRIDGE, MANCHESTER. BUILT 1829.

The world's first passenger railway station was in Liverpool Road and the bridge over Water Street, with its line branching off the main line to Piccadilly, still runs to the site. The main line bridge is seen in the background. (PPC, L.N.W. Railway, 1905.)

THE MANCHESTER SHIP CANAL COMPANY

ORIGINAL SHARE CAPITAL £8,000,000

DIVIDED INTO 4,000,000 PERPETUAL £5 PER CENTUM
PREFERENCE SHARES OF £1 EACH AND 4,000,000 ORDINARY SHARES OF £1 EACH.

By the Manchester Ship Canal (Finance) Act 1904 the Company are empowered from time to time to issue to the Corporation of Manchester 'Manchester Ship Canal Corporation Three and a half per centum Preference Shares'(or Preference Stock) equivalent in nominal amount to and in full satisfaction and discharge of all arrears of interest on the Corporation Debentures in the manner prescribed by the said Act and having priority over the Companys Original Preference and Ordinary Shares. Section 12 of the Manchester Ship Canal (Finance) Act 1904 provides that: 'All profits of the Company after payment of the dividends on Corporation Preference Shares and Corporation Preference Stock shall notwithstanding anything contained in any of the recited Acts or other Acts relating to the Company be divisible as follows:-Two-thirds to the holders of the Preference Shares issued in pursuance of the powers of the Acts of 1885 and 1887. One-third to the Ordinary Shareholders, provided that when the said two -thirds due to the holders of the Preference Shares issued in pursuance of the powers of the Acts of 1885 and 1887 shall in any year amount to Two Hundred Thousand Pounds all the remaining profits of that year shall be payable to the Ordinary Shareholders.'
The Manchester Ship Canal Act 1887 provides that if in any year ending on the thirty-first day of December there are not profits available for the payment of the full amount of dividend on the Preference Shares in respect of that year no part of the deficiency shall be made good out of the profits of any subsequent year or out of any other funds of the Company.

CERTIFICATE OF "MANCHESTER SHIP CANAL ORDINARY SHARES".

This is to Certify that *Catherine Theresa Wild* of *6 Vincombe Street, Hillhead, Glasgow* is the proprietor of *Twenty* Ordinary Shares numbered *7603511 to 7603530* inclusive of The Manchester Ship Canal Company subject to the provisions of the Acts relating to and the regulations of the said Company and that the sum of £1 has been paid upon each of the said Shares

Given under the Common Seal of the said Company the 30th day of October 1926

DIRECTOR.
SECRETARY.

NO TRANSFER OF THESE SHARES CAN BE MADE WITHOUT THE PRODUCTION OF THIS CERTIFICATE.

The Manchester Ship Canal was almost entirely in Salford and Stretford, but was run from Ship Canal House in King Street and was, in every way, a Manchester enterprise, built in the face of many years of opposition and derision. It opened to traffic in 1894 and until recently made Manchester a very busy inland port. The building of the Canal was a source of great local pride and countless "ordinary" people became small shareholders. The Company became the subject of a ferocious takeover battle in the eighties. Pomona Docks were mainly in Stretford territory and the early postcard view shows No. 2 Dock, with the ferries doing good business. (PPC, Blum & Degen, c.1900; Share Certificate, 1924.)

Peter Street has a famous history, being the site of the so-called Peterloo Massacre, a few years after Waterloo. Looking from the top of the street, across Mount Street, the Y.M.C.A., Theatre Royal and Free Trade Hall are in line down the left side. Across from them, the canopy of Miss Horniman's Gaiety Theatre can be seen behind the street lamp and tram standards. The building in the right foreground was demolished when the Central Library was built. The Friends' Institute building beyond came down more recently, to be replaced by an office block called Television House. (PPC, Valentine 69463, 1909.)

The Y.M.C.A., a massive building in red terracotta, on the corner of Mount Street, was recently refurbished for letting as offices. The Theatre Royal, beyond, became a cinema in the twenties, as did the Gaiety, a theatre internationally famous in the days of Miss Horniman. (PPC, Grosvenor Series 47, c.1910.)

The Swimming Bath at the Y.M.C.A., where, on the top floor, there was a well-equipped gymnasium with an indoor running track. (PPC, Philip G. Hunt, London.)

The Free Trade Hall. Manchester was the home of the Free Trade movement and the Hall was where many historic speeches were heard from leading politicians. In this 1903 picture Lloyd George is billed to speak (all tickets 2/-) and "Hamilton's Excursions" with "11 LIONS" are due on 27 July. The Hall was gutted in the blitz but restored afterwards. It was long the traditional home of the Halle Orchestra. (PPC, Vine Series 82.)

Oxford Street, at its beginning. The Odeon was still the Paramount, and new when the photograph was taken in 1932. Some live entertainment was still common on the programme, as shown on the poster. The Plaza Ballroom offers table tennis and billiards, besides summer dancing. At Portland Street the rounded corner of Petty & Jones' warehouse comes before the long frontage of the Calico Printers' building, with the Refuge Assurance tower beyond. Oxford Street became one-way, into town, in 1938. (PPCs: Paramount Service advertising card; Valentine 216659.)

Oxford Street, Manchester

IV 71941

A look up the street long before the Gaumont replaced the Hippodrome, with the Princes Theatre in the distance announcing the last week of *The Mousmé*. The delivery boy with his barrow is at the corner of Bridgewater Street. It is 1909 and, for haulage, the horse is still supreme in the city streets. A sign on the lamp post tells pedestrians to "KEEP RIGHT," but no-one is taking any notice. (PPC, Valentine 71941.)

OXFORD ROAD, MANCHESTER.   G.7695

The same scene thirty years on. The Gaumont was a typical city centre super cinema of its time, with a single, vast auditorium, restaurant and cafe, "Long Bar" and enormous queues on a Saturday night. The photograph was taken in 1938. "Cepea Fabrics" are advertised under the clock, on the Calico Printers' building and the Palatine Cafe is a little further up the street. There were other cinemas here in the thirties besides the big two and at the top of the street there was also the Princes Theatre. There were the New Oxford Cinema (seen just beyond the Gaumont) which uniquely was said to have two screens showing the same programme, and the Manchester News Theatre, which sometimes showed all-cartoon programmes, to the delight of its juvenile patrons, while a glance up Whitworth Street West would have revealed the Tatler, a small, luxurious (arm chair comfort) news cinema, now the Cornerhouse Cinema. The 1939 Guide Book compares the smaller cinemas to the super ones as "minnows among the tritons." "Tritons?" (PPC, Valentine G7695.)

Watts & Company's elaborately decorated warehouse in Portland Street is seen here, looking towards Piccadilly, some way along from Oxford Street in the 1920's. It was built in 1851 in such unrestrained magnificence as befitted Manchester's pre-eminence in the world of textiles. These warehouses were not merely for storage, but dignified premises for displaying the company's products to important customers.

St James Hall, with its prominent clock tower was one of Manchester's earliest venues for the "moving pictures." It was replaced by the Calico Printers' building. (PPC, A.H. & S.M., c.1904.)

Oxford Street at the Whitworth Street corner, with the Palace Theatre on the right and the old St Mary's Hospital on the left. (PPC, Valentine, c.1904.)

The Palace Theatre has survived the decline of music-hall to become the place for big productions, opera, musicals, ballet. The Calico Printers' great building is seen to good effect beyond it. Messrs. A. Drapkin is agent for "Best Policy" and "Foyer" cigarettes. The latter were surely the ones to smoke in the interval. (PPC, anon. P6, 1920's.)

It is 1932 and George Formby is playing the Hippodrome. The railway bridge is seen dividing Oxford Street from Oxford Road and the Refuge clock stands at a quarter to six. The message on this postcard reads, "elevated electric crosses bridge shown over." The service had just started. "All Inward Cars Stop Here" is suspended from the span wires above the 27D tram. Manchester's habit of hanging tram stop signs in mid-air rather disconcerted some visitors who were used to finding them nearer eye level.

Five

Around Albert Square

Albert Square, as it is today, exists because it was a handy, newly-cleared space to give a home to the late Prince Consort's Memorial in 1862. A mock-up had been tried in Piccadilly, beside Her Majesty, but it was felt that the design clashed with the style of the Royal Infirmary. They bothered about such things then. The rest of the Square was built round Prince Albert who appeared here before he did in London's Hyde Park. In spite of the obvious similarities in the design of the two Memorials, Sir George Gilbert Scott said that he had never seen the plans of Manchester's . Between here and St Peter's Square are the three great civic buildings. Mount Street, connecting the Squares, runs to G-MEX, the reborn Central Station, and the Holiday Inn, which will surely be known as "The Midland" for years to come, adds another landmark to the group. All of these survived the war, and the post-war planners, virtually unscathed. Princes Street runs alongside the Town Hall towards Chorlton-on-Medlock, passing another of the city's most treasured buildings, the Art Gallery in Mosley Street.

Central Station in Edwardian days. Lower Mosley Street is on the left. Mid-morning, but it is still quite a busy scene. Oddly, re-touching of the photograph has given the front of the arch, and the clock, a modernistic look more reminiscent of the thirties (cf. the picture opposite.) (PPC, Grosvenor 5, c.1907.)

The Midland was a flagship railway hotel, seen here from the station forecourt. A covered walkway across Windmill Street took passengers into the hotel, but soon the Peter Street entrance became the way in for most guests. Until recently it had no competition as the city's number one hotel, but it has never been thought of as an architectural gem. Like many Manchester buildings, it is faced in terracotta. (PPC, Davidson Bros., London 5007-4, c.1905.)

Central Station at about the war's end. The bus, labelled "Forces Only," carried the many servicemen and women crossing between the stations in those days, often with heavy and unwieldy kit bags. *Picture Post* was still with us, but not yet "British Railways." The Cheshire Lines was an old company whose name was kept for convenience after it was taken into joint ownership by the two big ones. (PPC, Richter, 61697)

LIBRARY AND NEW TOWN HALL EXTENSION, MANCHESTER.   G. 7477.

The Central Library and the Town Hall Extension were new when this photograph was taken in 1937 and, in fact, work on the latter was still being completed. The Library, opened in 1934 was built "in the tradition of the Early English Renaissance," and the Extension very successfully bridged the gap between it and the Town Hall. (PPC, Valentine G7477.)

ST. PETER'S SQUARE, SHOWING CENOTAPH AND TOWN HALL, MANCHESTER   M 232

The Library and Extension here show the effect of many years' soot deposition. The city centre had been a smoke-free zone already for several years before 1960, the date of this picture. Recent stone cleaning has made things bright again. (PPC, Valentine M232.)

The Great Hall, seen here new, was given state-of-the art facilities, but the echo was surely predictable. (PPC, AHC 1600, 1934.)

The King and Queen visited Manchester on a hot summer day, 17 July 1934, to be greeted by the vast crowds who then turned out on such occasions. As well as formally opening the Central Library, George V presented new drums to the Manchester Regiment, in front of the Town Hall. (PPC, AHC.)

The Central Library was the most important city centre building put up since the Town Hall seventy years earlier. It took four years to build and seen here is nearly ready. As well as building methods of the time, there are various period advertisments to admire. The later of the photographs also gives a good view of the surroundings: the Midland Hotel behind, the Friends' Meeting House in Mount Street on the right and the Gaiety Cinema's rear (seats 6d., 7d., 9d. and 1/-). The roofs in the foreground will soon disappear, when the Town Hall Extension is started. (Photographs courtesy of the City Engineer, February and May 1933.)

Between the Extension on the right and Dickenson Street corner on the left, Albert Square comes into view at the end of Mount Street. The Scottish Widows' building at the corner of the Square has its basement windows protected against bomb blast by brick walls; earlier in the war it would have been sandbags. Three people seem to be thinking of going into Ridgway's cafe there, beside the office of the National Savings Movement at No. 4. In the distance, a Stockport Corporation tram waits at its terminus. (PPC, Richter 61679, c.1945.)

The "Viaducts" connect the Town Hall with its Extension. The view is from Cooper Street towards Albert Square. (PPC, Richter, 616700.)

The Town Hall was built in 1868. Admirers of Victorian architecture cannot fail to be moved by its extravagance, so it is now more favourably looked on than it once was, though many think it looked better with its coat of soot. The 1939 City Guide refers sourly to its "gloomily magnificent style" but the 1995 Visitor Guide gives it pride of place on the cover. Mr Alfred Waterhouse, whose tour-de-force the building was, later developed such a passion for blood-red terracotta in his buildings that some people called him Alfred Slaughterhouse. (PPC, Valentine 98524, 1926.)

The Albert Memorial in an early Edwardian scene. The other worthies are Oliver Heywood, left, John Bright, centre and Bishop James Fraser in the distance. (PPC, Grosvenor 24.)

Albert Square in 1937. The clean Extension and Library contrast with the Town Hall. Plenty of waiting taxis but not a lot of other traffic, apart from the trams, which are already being steadily replaced by buses. (PPC, Valentine G7696.)

LBERT SQUARE, MANCHESTER.

In this view across the Square, Cross Street goes off at an angle in the left background, while on the right , a tram is entering from Princes Street, passing Clarence Street. Princes Street became one-way in 1938, and has been ever since. The prominent Midland Bank building, newly completed, is on the skyline while the flat-arched openings above the sun-blinds directly opposite us mark the site of one of Joe Lyons' tea rooms. (PPC, Excel Series 34, c.1936.)

MOSLEY STREET, MANCHESTER.   98531.

The City Art Gallery, in Mosley Street, was built in 1824 and the Extension, originally the Atheneum, next door in Princes Street, followed in 1837, both designed by Sir Charles Barry. A fine view along Princes Street shows both on a quiet afternoon in 1904. Mosley Street, stretching up to Piccadilly, is more clearly seen in the twenties photograph in which the policeman is waving two cars across the junction, while a 27 tram for Old Trafford comes up behind on its single track. J.Nightingale & Co., plumbers and sanitary engineers, are opposite the Gallery and the Kingston Restaurant is beyond. Hats are *de rigueur* for both sexes, cloth caps for the workers, bowlers for the businessmen, and a couple of wide-brimmed soft hats are on show too. A policeman is also present in the close-up view of the Gallery, in conversation with the crossing sweeper, while a nondescript bunch, including two telegraph boys, pose on the corner, or could they be trolley boys, the third crew-members on the trams until the thirties? An exhibition of watercolours is on view, free of charge. (PPCs: Valentine 98531, 1926; S.Hildesheimer & Co.; Schwerdtfeger, 0196.)

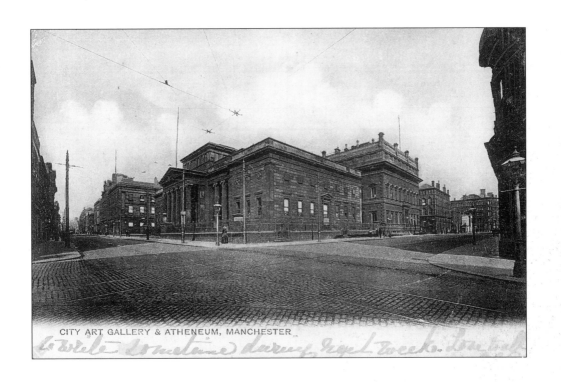

CITY ART GALLERY & ATHENEUM, MANCHESTER

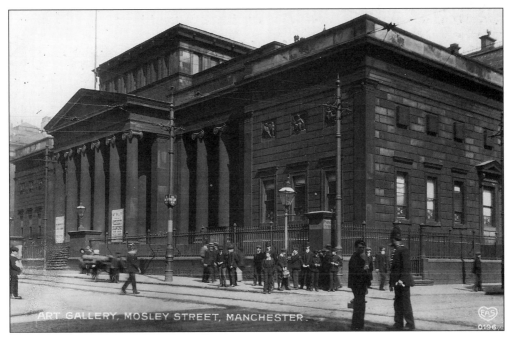

ART GALLERY, MOSLEY STREET, MANCHESTER.

DESIGN FOR THE NEW ART GALLERY,
PICCADILLY, MANCHESTER
BY ERNEST BERRY WEBBER, A.R.I.B.A

VISTA THROUGH THE SCULPTURE HALL
TOWARDS THE HALL OF MEMORY

The Art Gallery that never was. Plans to build it in Piccadilly were still awaiting funding in 1939 and were never revived after the war.

St Peter's, built in the eighteenth century and pulled down in 1907, is seen a few years before it went, to be replaced by a monument. Passing the church is a horse tram, followed, just in the picture, by a horse bus. The Restaurant Continental is at the Peter Street corner, next door to Mr G. Kretchy , the tailor. (PPC, Valentine c.1900.)

St Peter's Square about 1910. In front of the Town Hall clock tower is the terrace which was removed in the thirties, when the Central Library and Extension were built. A wagonette stands outside the Metro Cafe, next door to the A.A. & M.U. office. "My Valet" and "James Medical Warehouse" complete the row. (PPC, J.H. Ltd. 24741.)

The Cenotaph was erected in 1924, and the photograph was taken in that year. There is a hearse parked beside it, and wreaths have been laid. The Midland Hotel, fortress-like, is the backdrop to the scene. An advertisement for "Veno's," illuminated at night, is on a rooftop on the right. The top end of Oxford Street had, before the war, one of the best shows of neon signs in the city. The building on the corner of Lower Mosley Street was a casualty of the blitz, together with the Princes Theatre, which had already closed. (PPC, Valentine 92542, 1924.)

The Rose Garden on the roof of the Midland Hotel. On sunny days the view would be extensive but on this occasion it looks to have been a good way to get above the fog. Fog was a regular problem, as in many other cities, until the fifties and Manchester was a pioneer in smoke abatement. The Town Hall tower looms behind the waiter and the gent in the bowler. On the back of this postcard, the sender has written "I wonder if this is Bertie," but we shall never know if it *was* Bertie on that day in 1905. (PPC, Grosvenor Series.)

Six

Young Mancunians

The happiest days of our life. Well, perhaps, or perhaps not. No matter, children are resilient and images from the past, whatever the circumstances, usually show smiling faces or signs of earnest endeavour. Though the odd wistful or even melancholy look suggests that not all can dissemble at the photographer's command. Manchester's ancient Grammar School has never lost its reputation for excellence and Chetham's, still in the medieval home of the old Hospital and Blue Coat School, is now one of the country's leading music schools. As well as the famous independent ones, the city's local authority schools, growing in number and strength after the passing of the Education Acts last century, ensured that Manchester's young citizens were given a good start in life. In many parts of the city, though, poor housing and low, or almost non-existent income, meant that charities played a big part in helping to clothe and feed the children in the earlier years of the century and the Cinderella Club was one of these. Few aspects of life have shown so much outward change this century as the way young people are perceived, treated and educated. And how they dress!

Chetham's College has roots in the reign of Henry VI when the original buildings, still occupied, were built. The Bluecoat School was founded by Humphrey Chetham, of Crumpsall, in 1651 for "the education, maintenance and apprenticeship of boys requiring a start in life." Musical promise and talent gain admittance nowadays and Chetham's School of Music is internationally famous. (PPC, Grosvenor 31, 1904.)

The traditional Bluecoat uniform did not long survive the war. (PPC, AHC 2986, mid-thirties.)

Manchester Grammar School, about 1903. These old buildings in Long Millgate were abandoned in 1931, for they were by then unsuitable for an expanding, progressive school such as it had become and, as the school song put it, the Owl (the school emblem, an heraldic pun on the name of the founder, Hugh Oldham) "opened his wings and" flew "to a fairer, greener part," Fallowfield. Long Millgate lay empty and unsold until a German bomb destroyed it in 1940. (PPC, Raphael Tuck & Sons, "Town & City" 2009.)

A classroom at the Grammar School. Eton collars are worn by most of the boys and a variety of dead birds are displayed in glass cases at the back. (PPC, Marshall, Keene & Co., Edwardian.)

The High Master's Room. J.L. Paton was High Master from 1903 until 1924, and he ensured that the school kept pace with the enormous changes taking place in the world outside, and survived the grim days of the war. A believer in working and playing hard, he also established the summer treks for which the school became well-known.

The Grammar School's main door in Long Millgate. The School motto "Sapere Aude" ("Dare to be Wise") appears beneath the School name.

Manual Training Department: woodworking. The pupil in the foreground seems to be working on the hull of a model yacht, while an abacus lies on the next bench.

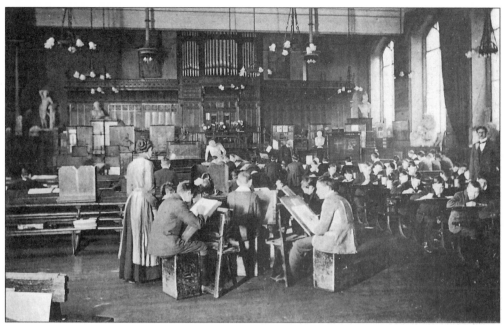

The Drawing Hall. Miss Edith Whitworth, the Art Mistress, oversees the still-life work in the foreground, while another form is hard at work at their desks. (PPCs, Marshall Keane.)

Douglas Gordon Miller, son of a Glasgow merchant, succeeded J.L. Paton as High Master in 1924, retiring in 1945, having seen the School's academic renown rise to new heights after the successful move from the city centre in 1931. Born Douglas Schulze, he was an Oxford Blue and he played rugby for Scotland. He changed his name during World War One while Rector of Kelvinside Academy in his native city. He was known for his quiet courtesy combined with a determination to protect the interests of the School, shown most notably in his decision to end the unworkable evacuation to Blackpool in 1939, despite strong official disapproval.

Waterloo Road School served the Strangeways district. Near the junction with Great Ducie Street, on the corner of Marian Street, it was the dominant building in the area for many years. Notice-boards quote the Education Acts of 1870-90 and the Technical Education Acts in advertising the "Commercial Evening School" and the "Science & Art Evening School." The present Cheetwood Primary School, in its place, is somewhat less over-powering. (Photograph courtesy of the City Engineer, 1906.)

Princess Road Municipal School in Moss Side. The boys here are enjoying a stay at the Manchester Country School in 1908. A great variety of dress, but still plenty of Eton collars can be seen here, and a fascinating range of expressions.

The Whit Walks in Manchester and around were a tradition which remained strong until the Second World War. The churches of different denominations held walks on their own days. This one, on Whit Friday, is from St Wilfrid's in Hulme in Edwardian days. As can be seen, huge crowds turned out.

Ready for the walk, a group of happy girls (and one little brother on the front row, looking less than thrilled to be seen in such company) captured by photographer Edgar Morgan of 2a Alexandra Road, between the wars.

A kerbside waif in 1912. The Cinderella Club was founded in 1889, "to brighten the lives of poor children" and it went on doing this for fifty years before being merged with war charities. Patrons included the Earl and Countess of Derby and the civic heads , and their wives, of Manchester and Salford. Fund raising efforts, apart from collections, included doll dressing on a massive scale. The good works, such as providing much-needed food and clothing, culminated in a summer camp at St Anne's-on-Sea where 120 children each week enjoyed the sea breezes. The Club was sponsored by the *Daily Dispatch* and *Evening Chronicle*.

DIET TABLE.

	Breakfast, 8 a.m.	Dinner, 12-30 p.m.	Tea, 5 p.m.	Supper, 8-30 p.m.
SUNDAY.......	Porridge, Syrup, Milk, Bread and Butter	Roast Beef, Potatoes, Rice Pudding	Bread and Butter, Tea	Bread and Syrup, Milk
MONDAY	Porridge, Syrup, Milk, Bread and Butter	Pea Soup, Suet Pudding, Syrup	Bread and Butter, Cocoa	Bread and Dripping, Milk
TUESDAY	Porridge, Syrup, Milk, Bread and Butter	Hot Pot, Rice Pudding	Bread and Butter, Tea	Bread and Butter, Milk
WEDNESDAY..	Porridge, Syrup, Milk, Bread and Butter	Pea Soup, Suet Pudding with Currants	Bread and Butter, Cocoa	Bread and Syrup, Milk
THURSDAY ...	Porridge, Syrup, Milk, Bread and Butter	Hot Pot, Rice Pudding	Bread and Butter, Tea	Bread and Dripping, Milk
FRIDAY.......	Porridge, Syrup, Milk, Bread and Butter	Pea Soup, Suet Pudding, Syrup	Bread and Butter, Cocoa	Bread and Butter, Milk
SATURDAY....	Porridge, Syrup, Milk, Bread and Butter	CAMP EMPTY	Bread and Butter, Tea	Bread and Syrup or Dripping, Milk

Any Scraps of Bread there may be are used for Puddings

The Diet for the campers. It would be better than they were used to for the rest of the year, but a modern children's dietitian would not give it many marks.

Boys "seeing their comrades off to camp" and "hoping their turn will come."

ON THE WAY TO THE STATION.
En route to the Camp.

En route to the Camp. The crocodile marches along a very wet Victoria Street on its way to Exchange Station. (Photographs from Club brochure, 1913.)

THE MANCHESTER GIRLS' HIGH SCHOOL,
DOVER STREET.   J.L.B.SERIES,
100

The Manchester High School for Girls, now to be found in Rusholme, was founded in 1874, thanks to the efforts of leading citizens "to provide for Manchester's daughters what has been provided without stint for Manchester's sons." From an initial 60 pupils it soon grew and moved from two converted houses in Oxford Road to its own place in Dover Street. Miss Elizabeth Day, the first Head Mistress was succeeded by Miss Sarah A. Burstall, in 1898 and she proved to be a pioneering spirit whose new ideas, put into practice before she retired in 1924, brought the School the high repute it still enjoys. The move into new, uncompleted buildings at Grangethorpe, took place in September 1940, just in time to see them destroyed in the blitz. The return to a new School took place in 1949. A chemistry lesson is in progress in an early photograph. A proper emphasis on Science was one of Miss Burstall's most important innovations. (PPC, JLB 100, 1923; card and photograph courtesy of Manchester High School for Girls.)

Form 3A, in March 1917, are looking very jolly, in spite of the hard times.

Miss Burstall is seated beside Miss Caress in this 1913 form photograph of IVa Upper. Top Row:-J.Ramsell, M.Griffiths, Y.Addiman, J.Stewart, F.Wells, E.Backhouse. Middle row: L.Bruce, E.Walker, D.Walthew, E.Bird, F.Wood, D.Samuels, N.Williamson. Front row: K.Winder, E.Snowdon, M.Eastwood, M.Robohn, W.Scotson. (PPCs, Ward, courtesy of Manchester High School for Girls.)

The Inter-School Sports Day and, unfortunately, it's raining again. The supporters lining the track watch while a race is organised.

Get ready, get set ..., though the boy with the crinkly top seems quite relaxed about it.

The Obstacle Race was always good for a laugh. Under the bar go the boys and then through the horse collars – not so many old tyres to spare in those days.

The little girls are not exactly dressed for speed, and the one on the left looks as though she just might make a false start. (PPCs: R.Banks, 37 Fountain Street, Manchester, c.1912.)

Seven

Strangeways, Cheetham and Hightown

Beyond the bridge at Exchange was always a different world. Along Great Ducie Street, mean shops and slum housing replaced the busy city centre, the scene relieved only by the Victorian Assize Courts and the gaol, its tower a landmark for miles. A sizable Jewish community was already living in Strangeways even before the pogroms in eastern Europe in the eighties and after. Novels by authors such as Louis Golding, Howard Spring and, recently, Maisie Mosco, tell graphically of their life, the early struggles, migration up to Hightown and beyond and then dispersal to the outer suburbs, to be succeeded often by new citizens of different faiths. Of the numerous synagogues, only one small congregation now remains in the area. Between Waterloo Road and Cheetham Hill Road (York Street then) was once rural Cheetwood where earlier last century "loving couples would find their way" to take tea in gardens "gay with numerous flowers," the air "sweet with their perfume." But brickfields and sour, bare earth replaced Cheetwood's charms, followed by the raincoat and other garment factories for which this part became famous. On the main road through Cheetham, the Town Hall, the Assembly Rooms and churches and synagogues were the landmarks in a generally dreary scene. Near Elizabeth Street was the Riviera Cinema, always referred to as the "Riveera," even after it became the Odeon. Hightown, a compact district where Jew and Gentile lived their largely separate lives in reasonable harmony, in parallel streets of terraced housing, became unrecognisable after the post-war changes there.

Briddon Street runs between New Bridge Street and Southall Street, on the very edge of Strangeways. Kosher shops and eating places catering to the tastes of customers from different parts of Europe were to be found all over. Boddington's brewery is the main presence around here these days. (Photograph from *Walks in Jewry* by W.O.E Oesterley, 1901, courtesy of Manchester Jewish Museum.)

The Assize Courts were built in 1859. Alfred Waterhouse was the architect. It was to have had a rather odd clock tower, but instead a gable over the entrance was topped by a statue of Moses, the law giver. When the bomb-damaged building was taken down, Moses could not be saved and toppled to the ground. The Courts had been damaged in December 1940, when the Woolsack Hotel in Southall Street was destroyed, along with the little Futurist Cinema further up the street, but it was in the city's last major air raid the following May that it was totally wrecked. (PPC, Boots' Cash Chemists, 1907.)

The staff of the Women's Section at Strangeways have their whistles dangling at the ready. The sender of this cheery postcard, bearing Christmas & New Year Greetings, refrained from adding the traditional message, "Having a Wonderful Time, Wish You Were Here." (PPC, Percy Guttenberg, 1907.)

The Higham Factory at 127, Great Ducie Street, opposite the Assize Courts, made musical instruments and here a bit of silver plating is going on. (Advertising postcard, 1912.)

Park Street was first left off Cheetham Hill Road. Something seems to be going on, but there is no record of what. The 1884 Directory lists the following round the corner on the main road: Park Independent Chapel, Mr A. Poland, Ostrich Feather Merchant, Mr Salmon Delmar's boarding house and the Synagogue of the Congregation of British Jews. The Great Synagogue was just a little further along. (From *Walks in Jewry*, 1901, courtesy of Manchester Jewish Museum.)

60   MANCHESTER——MANSFIELD.

MANCHESTER.

KNOWSLEY HOTEL,

CHEETHAM HILL ROAD,

Only a few minutes' walk from Victoria Railway Station,

Will be found by Travellers who appreciate Good and Lofty Rooms, and enjoy the Quietude and Comfort which the noisy parts of the City cannot offer, a very acceptable house.

Omnibuses to all parts of the City pass the door every few minutes.

J. B. BRENMEHL, LESSEE.

SWAN HOTEL,

MANSFIELD.

UNDER the management of Miss WHITE, daughter of the late Robert White, for 30 years proprietor. The best centre for visiting Sherwood Forest, The "Dukeries," Welbeck, Thoresby, Clumber, Newstead, Hardwick, Bolsover, &c.

"The best plan is to get a carriage from the 'Swan' at Mansfield."— *Rambles among the Hills*, by Louis J. Jennings.

An Omnibus meets all Trains.

The Knowsley Hotel in Cheetham Hill Road, an advertisement from Black's *Guide to Scotland*. Like much else here, it has now gone, but it survived into the second half of the century.

Mr Rosenberg's butchers shop at 133, Bury New Road, just past Broughton Lane, between Grove Street and Norfolk Street, and very nearly over the border into Salford. Telephone 153, Higher Broughton, in the late twenties perhaps, before dials, let alone push-button phones and 11-digit numbers arrived. (Photograph courtesy of Manchester Jewish Museum.)

Kendal & Jacobs' factory in Derby Street makes underwear and nightgowns and here it is December 1930. The workforce in this Jewish owned business, as in others, is mixed, so work is laid aside this afternoon for the Christmas party. Seen in the foreground, at their Singer machines, are Minnie Solomon and Marjorie Carr. (Photograph courtesy of Manchester Jewish Museum.)

Mr Graingold's shop opposite the Town Hall in 1927. Among the over-the-counter remedies on sale are "Meggezones" and "Steedman's Powders," for cross and teething babies, an old favourite in spite of the toxic mercury they then contained. (Photograph courtesy of Manchester Jewish Museum.)

Simon Blaiwais stands in the doorway of his fur shop in Cheetham Hill Road, in the early nineteen hundreds. It is opposite St Chad's Church, a little lower down than Cheetham Town Hall. Above the window are displayed two medals awarded in Poland in, possibly, happier days. The workroom window is open, so it must be not a bad day. (Photograph courtesy of Manchester Jewish Museum.)

The Victoria Jewish Memorial Hospital, always non-sectarian, opened in 1904 in Sherborne Street, off Elizabeth Street. The Out-Patients, added in 1908, is now the only part open. The hospital was hit in the blitz, while casualties from nearby were being treated, and five members of staff were killed. (Photograph courtesy of Manchester Jewish Museum.)

After the steep rise from Strangeways, Waterloo Road flattens out as it reaches Hightown. Elizabeth Street, once known, no doubt with good reason, as Dirty Lane, crosses in the foreground in this view looking up the road. The Wilton Arms is on the left; the public house on the other corner survives to this day as the Waterloo. (PPC, Grosvenor 53, 1905.)

SYCAMORE STREET HIGHTOWN 264

Sycamore Street, five along on the right-hand side from Elizabeth Street, was one of ten in Hightown named after trees. It was 1906 when this view was taken and the young Louis Golding had been living here since the family split up over a dispute about religious practices. Sycamore Street was the model for *Magnolia Street* in his novel of that name. He recorded that it was unique in that all the Jews lived in the odd-numbered houses and the Gentiles in the even. The small boys are on the Gentile side and the toddlers on the Jewish, here, looking from Waterloo Road towards Herbert Street. This style of housing dates from 1870-90, cf. Hibbert Street, p.142, more typical of an earlier period. (PPC, anon. 264.)

Bignor Street, higher up Waterloo Road, was built later than Sycamore Street, with gardens and other luxuries for the tenants. It then ran the whole way to Cheetham Hill Road, and St Luke's Parish Church is seen in the distance. Nowadays it ends at Heywood Street. (PPC, JLB, c.1910.)

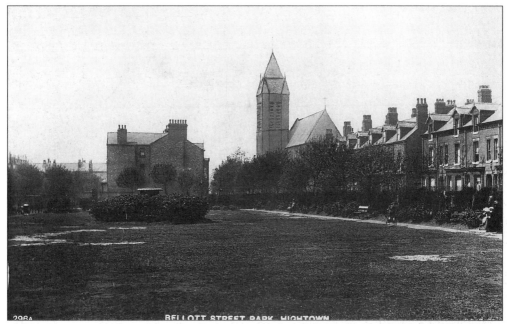

Bellott Street is another of the very few survivors of pre-war Hightown. Its little park has been enlarged since Bignor Street was shortened. The street used to continue across Waterloo Road as Bellott Street West and very soon after became Walnut Street, Salford. Walnut Street was devastated, and many lives lost, in one of the first "incidents" on 22 December 1940. (PPC, JLB, c.1910.)

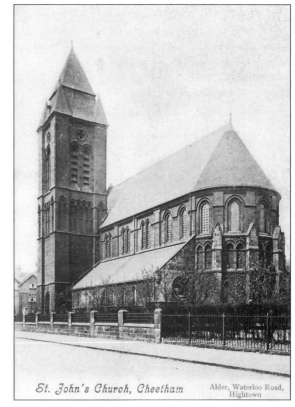

The Church of St John the Evangelist, between Bellott Street and Brideoak Street, was designed by Edward Paley, the architect of Rylands Library. The view is from Bellott Street, towards Waterloo Road. It is one of the few prominent buildings of old Hightown to survive. (PPC, Valentine, for Alder, Waterloo Road, 1904.)

121

The Cheetham Cricket Club's ground marked the outer limit of Hightown. Those living higher up Waterloo Road preferred to think of themselves as being in Cheetham Hill, a more desirable address. The Central Synagogue in Heywood Street, with its squat tower, is seen across the field, with the Convent buildings to the right. St Luke's Church spire is on the left skyline. A peaceful, sunny Saturday afternoon, with a match in progress. It is June 1940 and more momentous events are taking place elsewhere. Nowadays the Synagogue, the Church and the Convent are no more and the cricket ground is a housing estate. In the forties, though, it had its day of fame. During a match on 9 August 1947 a straight drive went for six, clearing the fence, at that point seventeen feet higher than the pitch, and hit the head of a Miss Stone who was standing outside her house in Beckenham Road, seen here off Waterloo Road. The action for damages ended in an appeal to the House of Lords, where their Lordships came to the conclusion the no-one was really to blame. The ruling set a precedent for judgments in circumstances where such unhappy consequences could not reasonably be foreseen. There is no record of whether the ball was recovered. (Photograph by the author.)

Eight

From New Cross to Ardwick

East of the city centre, main roads radiate to the towns around, in Lancashire and Cheshire, in an arc stretching from Miller Street to Ardwick Green. Names such as Ancoats, Miles Platting and Ardwick itself (once a favoured residential address) are reminders of the villages that were once here. Last century saw the area become an unlovely place of industry and crowded housing, railway lines to take the traffic from the old canals, and very little greenery. The River Medlock ran through Philips Park, but the gas works in the area contributed more to the atmosphere there. Some early attempts were seen to provide better housing for those in the slums. At first, though, to set too high a standard for the working class was not advised. Provide "no wooden skirtings, which might be used for firewood; no fresh-air inlets - the working man would block them up; no baths as there are plenty of public ones; it is no great hardship for members of this class to share a scullery with other families." Such was the advice of the London architect responsible for the Victoria Square flats at New Cross in 1889, and the advice was accepted. Some, it is fair to add, thought the advice "reactionary".

Flats in Rochdale Road, an uncommon style of housing in Manchester at the time. Sudell Street, on the right, is about a quarter of a mile from the start of the road at Shude Hill. It is 1938. The tram track has been tarred over and the trolley bus has replaced the tram. At the bus stop a sign warns of a railway crossing, and the *Evening Chronicle* bill tells of "British Soldiers Killed in Palestine." The *Manchester Guardian* has another tragic item: "Runaway Pit Train, Four Killed." A.Blasgies, Tailor, has premises at the corner, with Sydney Smith & Co. above him. (Photograph courtesy of City Engineer.)

No. 27 Westmorland Street, Harpurhey on 18 July 1938, but a scene which might be almost anywhere near Manchester city centre. Next door the brickwork has been re-pointed and chalk marks suggest No. 27 is to get the same treatment. The freshly whitestoned steps and the spotless lace curtains are the rule, rather than the exception, the mark of houseproud tenants. The kitten at No. 27, though, looks happier than the man at 29. (Photograph courtesy of City Engineer.)

Victoria Square, on Oldham Road, at New Cross, has a grand appearance which belies the basic amenities thought good enough for the tenants when it was put up in 1889, as mentioned on p.123. In 1938, planned conversions to provide bathrooms and separate kitchens had not yet taken place. Spittal Street is on the right, with Thompson Street opposite. As well as "Hovis" and cameras, you can get a permanent wave here or a 9yd. x 12yd. carpet for 45 shillings (£2.25.) (Photograph courtesy of City Engineer.)

Chester Street, Miles Platting, in 1900. A short cul-de-sac off Oldham Road, backing onto the railway, it looks very neat and clean in this view, taken to record completed improvements. All the brickwork is new and free of soot. The family who live on the right have made quite a garden on their balcony. (Photograph courtesy of City Engineer.)

Philips Park, between Oldham and Ashton New Roads, a green oasis in an industrial district, was well-cared for; the Medlock ran between it and the Cemetery. The message accompanying the view reads: "I am very pleased to hear you have got your new leg." (PPC, A.H. & S.M., 1909.)

Ashton Old Road at Grey Mare Lane in the early thirties, with the Grey Mare Hotel, a Threlfall's pub, on the right. Albert Wagstaff advertises his pianos and "His Master's Voice" gramophones. The scene shown here at this important junction is today unrecognisable. (PPC, Barrett & Co. 440.)

The Ardwick Empire, strategically placed at Ardwick Green, survived as a music hall well into the post-war years. Now known as the Apollo Theatre it is an important concert venue. (PPC, 1904.)

The Salvation Army Temple at the corner of Grosvenor Street and Greek Street, quite close to the Empire. A full programme is listed on the board in Greek Street. Harvest Thanksgiving, September 17, 18 & 19, is to be conducted by Major Garrie. (PPC, 1908.)

THE POLYGON   MANCHESTER   ARDWICK

Polygon Street is a short passage between Brunswick Street and Stockport Road, which the shops face. From the right, Hartley the draper is at the corner, next door to Wm. Slack, agent for Pullars of Perth. His window is crammed with Raphael Tuck's picture postcards, the craze for collecting them being then near its height. Meeson's, the sweet shop, has moved away, which may be why the two boys on the tricycle are looking a bit unhappy. Meeson's gimmick at one time was to give you double the quantity you paid for. The Polygon Cigar Store offers "Casket Cigarettes" at 3d. a packet, a name which might nowadays be regarded as off-putting. James Coombes & Co. have their familiar blue shop front listing over eighty branches where gents' boots are soled and heeled for 2/6d. (12½ p.) "A Big Trade and Small Profits" was their slogan. Further along, a bike would cost you five guineas. (PPC, 1908.)

HYDE ROAD TRAM DEPOT. MANCHESTER.

Hyde Road Tram Depot and Works, opened in 1905, seen several years later. It served the system till the end. The tramways had been electrified at the turn of the century and soon became one of the biggest and best in the country, but failure to keep up with modern developments in the thirties led to them being abandoned in favour of the cheaper and more flexible bus. The war postponed their end from 1942 till January 1949. Now they have returned, in a different form! Looking towards town, Devonshire Street is between the depot and Nicholls Hospital. (PPC, JLB 224.)

The Manchester bogie tram in its ultimate form, seen here in Albert Square near the end of its life, in 1947. Built in 1927 and not bad looking in its cream and red livery, it was lacking even in such refinements as power brakes or a modern current collector to replace the trolley wheel. All trams carried the advertisement seen on the top front window, and also to be found on the inside saloon doors, "SHIP BY THE SHIP CANAL." (Photograph R.B.Parr Collection, courtesy of Tramway Museum Society, Crich.)

Trolleybuses came to Manchester on 1 March 1938, when they first ran along Ashton Old Road, in place of the trams, the City Council overruling the forceful General Manager, R. Stuart Pilcher, who always favoured the diesel bus. Although further routes followed, trolleybuses went out of fashion in Britain, and the city's last ran in 1966. Number 1215 dates from 1950, built by Crossley and seen standing in Parker Street. It ran until 1963.

Manchester Corporation bus 617 came from Crossley's, the local firm and was brand new when photographed here in 1937 in its original "streamline" livery, with the guard standing by. Tram 558, in the background, dated from 1932, one of the last batch built. Unlike the older trams, these were not consigned to the flames in 1949 but sold to roam the streets of cities as far apart as Leeds and Aberdeen for a further few years. (Photograph by Dr J. G. Stewart.)

The Decorated Tram. Important national and civic events were marked by fitting countless light bulbs outside and running the vehicle round the system in the evenings. Buses received the same treatment. The Civic Week in 1926 celebrated the Silver Jubilee of the system. (PPC, C. Urmston, Pendleton.)

Garibaldi Street, off Hyde Road, just before the bridge carrying the main line south from London Road. A damp morning in January 1939 and not an inspiring scene, or a lively one, but the streets are at least free of plastic litter and graffiti. Garibaldi Street disappeared in post-war redevelopment and the Italian hero is no longer commemorated anywhere in the city. (Photograph courtesy of City Engineer.)

Nine

South of the Centre

After dipping under the bridge past Whitworth Street, Oxford Road rises gently to All Saints. The 1945 plan would have closed Oxford Road there, to create a group of "Centres for Culture, Education and Medicine" in an area bounded by Upper Brook Street and Cambridge Street, with a great Civic Hall facing the city. The University of Manchester has been in Oxford Road since the days when it was Owen's College and the campus has spread as its fame and reputation has done likewise. With the Royal Infirmary and other hospitals in the area, and with the Royal Northern College of Music and the Whitworth Gallery here too, it is easy to follow the thinking of the post-war planners. West of here lie Hulme, whose narrow streets were among the most congested in the city, and Moss Side, a district which has had much bad publicity. On the other side of Oxford Road is Chorlton-on-Medlock. The River Medlock winds its way from Ben Brierley's much-loved Daisy Nook to enter the city at Clayton Bridge, on its path to the Irwell. Once there were cotton mills along its banks, beside the workers' homes, but the stream is pretty unnoticeable now. As Plymouth Grove stretches out towards Longsight and Stockport Road a more spacious residential part is reached.

Kirkmanshulme Lane in Longsight about 1910. Longsight Station is in the distance, where the roadway dips to go below the bridge. Quite a few residents are taking a stroll in the afternoon sunshine past the well-proportioned terraced houses. Nowadays this part of Kirkmanshulme Lane is part of a busy route cutting across the corner of Belle Vue and crossing Hyde Road. (PPC, Woodhey Series, A.H. & S.M.)

North Road, with Crowcroft Park on the left of the picture. Substantial Edwardian semi-villas overlooking the park to Stockport Road beyond. (PPC, H.Thorpe, Longsight, 1913.)

The Victoria Baths. High Street has become Hathersage Road these days, but the public baths, near the Plymouth Grove end, are still there, the brickwork cleaned beautifully, but the building, when last seen, was boarded up. (PPC, A.H. & S.M., 1908.)

Victoria Park was an exclusive place to live, with toll gates to discourage the merely curious. The entrance in Plymouth Grove was just down from Stockport Road. The bearded gate-keeper is chatting to one who doesn't look like a resident. Two notices lay down the Rules & Regulations decreed by the Victoria Park Trust while below them £5 is offered to the finder of a Diamond Cluster Ring. (PPC, JLB 119, 1926.)

Plymouth Grove, looking towards Upper Brook Street. The tram, bound for Albert Square from Stockport, is passing Swinton Grove and the tower of the Wesleyan Chapel is beyond. (PPC, Chas. Wilkinson 999, late 1920's.)

138

Upper Brook Street at the High Street crossing and the entrance to Victoria Park, from which the trams were barred until the twenties. Autumn Street opens in the right foreground, Summer and Spring having, naturally, preceded them. Winter Street was away in Strangeways. On the other side of the road were January to July. This whimsical array of street names has disappeared now, only February Street surviving. In front of the shops in Jubilee Terrace the billposts advertise the *Daily News* ("The Crisis, Unions Promise Support") and the *Dispatch* ("Burglars Amazing Ingenuity.") The Misses A. & A. West have the confectioner's at the corner, while further down those who fancy a smoke can buy Mexican cigars. (PPC, Grosvenor 93, 1910.)

Anson Road runs through Victoria Park and this 1926 view is from the Dickenson Road junction, with Kensington Road opening on the right. The toll gates were removed in the late thirties, many of the big houses remain, often adapted to other uses. (PPC, Valentine 98604.)

Swinton Grove opens off Upper Brook Street on the right, where the trams are passing each other. The church, whose spire is visible above the trees, remains, now the Holy Trinity Armenian Church. (PPC, JLB 106, 1924.)

All Saints Church, Manchester.

All Saints Church, another casualty of the blitz. By the 1930s, the graveyard had become a children's playground. Thirty years earlier, though, the monuments are undisturbed and there is a handsome drinking fountain on the pavement. Behind the church, on Lower Richmond Street, as it was, are the twin towers of the Presbyterian Church, next to the Ear Hospital and another church whose spire is seen. With the Congregational Chapel in Cavendish Street, beside Hulme Town Hall, the religious needs of the neighbourhood seemed to be well catered for. A peaceful scene at what was a busy junction; now the traffic on Mancunian Way passes close by and Cavendish Street no longer leads to what is left of Stretford Road. The open space has been kept, and the old cinema, off the picture on the left-hand side and, these days, a pub, on the corner of Grosvenor Street, is a well-preserved reminder of times past in these parts. (Boots Pelham Series.)

Hibbert Street, a little side street off City Road in Hulme, seen here in 1924. Not many amenities here, in housing dating from the middle of the last century. Not much traffic was expected either, on washing day. The post-war re-development in Hulme did not last as long as the houses shown here. (Photograph courtesy of City Engineer.)

Medlock Street, in Hulme, in 1934, with the Post Office at the corner of George Street. The local shops provide for all your daily needs. The Supper Bar for fish, chips & peas, the grocer for Lyon's Tea, Farrow's Mustard and Spratt's Ovals (this for the dog). A haircut and a shave at the Toilet Saloon next and then a few steps to the shop for Player's Navy Cut. You can also get "Coupons" here "For Sale at Lowest Prices." J.Bentley will repair your shoes and sell you Cherry Blossom to keep them smart. At the P.O. itself Wills's Gold Flake is promoted, as well as their "Four Aces" cigarettes - can anyone remember them? This site is now just about under the Mancunian Way but a short stretch of Medlock Street survives in name, as an important link with Princes Road. (Photograph courtesy of City Engineer.)

The Hulme Tug o' War team who pulled against Dalton in the 1917 contest. A husky looking lot to be available at that stage of the war. Were they on leave, or in reserved occupations? The Reverend and his lady stand behind the team, who seem to have won. (PPC, Ward.)

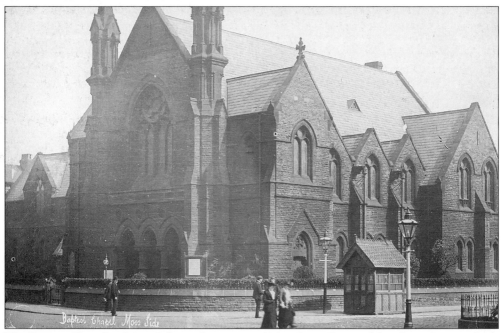

The Baptist Chapel in Moss Side, at the corner of Moss Lane East and Stockton Street, which is on the right of the picture. The wooden hut was one of many placed strategically for the benefit of Tramways employees.

Alexandra Road, Moss Side

Alexandra Road, at the heart of Moss Side, just along from the Baptist Chapel. Moss Lane West branches off to the right and Alexandra Road itself stretches away into the fog from its beginning here, past the Park to Wilbraham Road. T. Seymour Mead & Co., Tea & Provision Merchants, whose delivery vans stand outside their shop, was a famous name for many years to come. The posters in the shop windows are promoting their sausages, 7d. or 8d. a pound. The Alexandra Park Hotel is next door to the shop, followed by Slater's, advertising their self-raising flour. Meanwhile, on the other side of the road, J.R.Blair & Son promote their Celebrated Strathmore Scotch Whisky. Like most of Moss Side from this period, nothing in the scene remains as it was. (PPC, Thornton Series, Altrincham, early Edwardian.)

The Victoria University is the original name of the University of Manchester. Before that it was Owen's College. This view of the main building, with the Whitworth Hall facing Burlington Street, is from 1926. Oxford Road stretches away towards the city. The removal of the sooty coating from the buildings in post-war days has transformed their appearance. (PPC, Valentine 98520.)

y Union, on a damp and dismal day in 1912. Despite the city's moist reputation, an prove, by means of statistics, that it doesn't rain here more than anywhere else.

By the sixties, the Union building had been replaced by a block in Portakabin style, and the Union itself is a much more stylish modern building beside it. A Ford Anglia, with its unmistakable backward-sloping rear window, is passing a parked Austin A30. (PPC, courtesy of Dennis Print & Publishing, Scarborough; Bamforth & Co., 149.)

The Fabian Society in 1917. The Fabians, the socialist society founded in 1884, were well represented in the universities. The men are outnumbered, by four to thirteen. (PPC, Ward.)

The Students' Rag was always on Shrove Tuesday and the Rag Rag was on sale during the week before, likely as not to result in a letter to the *Guardian* from "Disgusted" of Alderley Edge. There is a splendid variety of costumes in this group photograph, including a skeleton smoking a pipe, The Reverend Spoil Sport at the back, and, inappropriately, Father Christmas. (PPC, Ward, 1912.)

M'c Students. Shrove Tuesday 1912

WARD . photo . L

This arresting study is also from a Ward's postcard.

The New Club, at the corner of Dover Street, backing on to the Manchester High School for Girls. The staff are at the door, while the members pose on the balcony. (PPC, c.1910.)

Wounded soldiers in the First World War, with their nurses, at the 2nd Western General Hospital, in the Ducie Street Schools, off Oxford Road. The chap taking his tea behind them probably didn't expect to be noticed eighty years later. (PPC, J.Cleworth, 26 September 1916.)

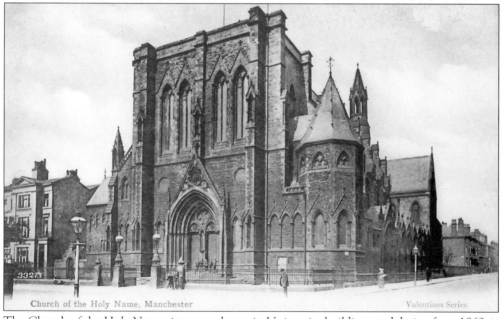

Church of the Holy Name, Manchester   Valentines Series

The Church of the Holy Name, just past the main University building, and dating from 1869, is here incomplete, lacking the upper part of the tower, added this century. The original plans had included a 240ft. spire. Ackers Street is seen on the right. J. A. Hansom, the architect, was a versatile man, inventing the Hansom Cab and also designing a memorial to the Duke of Sussex, to be put up in London, and described by Cecil Stewart as "utterly macabre and monstrous ... one of the most fascinating horrors of the age." It was never built. (PPC, Valentine, 1900.)

The Royal College of Music, in Ducie Street, between Ducie Grove and Brighton Street, built in the nineties, but now replaced with the spread of the University campus. The corner shop belongs to H. T. Barlow and sells, among other things, Wills's Woodbine cigarettes. One of the cheaper brands, then much favoured by message boys, they were libellously rumoured to be made from road sweepings, in the days when horses were the main contributors to that commodity. (PPC, Valentine 71763, 1909.)

Opposite: The Brodsky Quartette played an important part in the city's musical life for about a quarter of a century. Adolph Brodsky, a Russian Jew from Taganrog, was Leader of the New York Symphony Orchestra when Sir Charles Halle invited him to Manchester in 1895. His first appearance was at the Schiller-Anstalt in Nelson Street in November of that year. He was already celebrated as the man who had given the first public performance of Tchaikovsky's "unplayable" Concerto and although Halle died shortly afterwards, Brodsky so much preferred Manchester to New York that he made his home here. He founded the Quartette a few years later and regular concerts were given at Ducie Street. He was visiting Germany when the war broke out in 1914, but was repatriated thanks to pleas by Hamilton Harty, but Carl Fuchs was not so lucky, and did not return till 1919. Brodsky died in 1929, aged 78. The new Brodsky Quartet is well-established, but apart from the name, there is no direct connection. (PPC, Percy Guttenberg, 1904.)

PERCY GUTTENBERG.
Photo. MANCHESTER.

"BRODSKY QUARTETTE"

DR. BRODSKY   C. FUCHS   S. SPEELMAN   R. BRIGGS

The new Royal Infirmary, described in 1939 as "a veritable world of healing," was opened in 1909 by King Edward. It is seen here not long after opening. The line of carriages and the crowd of people suggest a special occasion, possibly to do with the opening. The hospital was damaged in 1940 on two occasions, with nurses and patients among the casualties. (PPC, A.H. & S.M.)

The Methodist Church in Oxford Road, here described as Dr Maclaren's, was at the entrance to York Place, between the Royal Infirmary and the new St Mary's Hospital. (PPC, Charles Voisey, London, Edwardian.)

Number 5, York Place was *not* the birth-place of David Lloyd George, and nor was his initial "E." As far as is known he was born at 5, New York Place in Chorlton-on-Medlock, not far from Ardwick Green (a block of flats is named in his honour there.) His father was a schoolmaster who had found employment in Manchester, and whose early death was blamed on the damp and smoky atmosphere! The York Place shown on this advertising postcard was in Oxford Road, a leafy place of substantial houses beyond the Royal Infirmary but is given in some biographies as the actual birthplace though Mr Kuenmann, a designer, who produced this advertising card, should surely have known better. (PPC, 1910.)

5, YORK PLACE,
Birth-place of Rt. Hon. E. Lloyd George, Chancellor of Exchequer now occupied by Albert A. Kuenemann, Designer.

The Royal Eye Hospital, next door to the Infirmary, at the corner of Nelson Street, was also severely damaged in the blitz, a hundred beds being lost. (PPC, anon.)

Whitworth Park, opposite the Infirmary and St Mary's, is viewed across the small lake, looking towards Oxford Road. The Art Gallery is behind the trees on the left. The Infirmary had not yet been built, but the Methodist church is prominent. (PPC, Rival Series, 1904.)

The front of the Whitworth Gallery, facing Oxford Road, around 1910. Founded in 1892, it is famous for its collection of watercolours. (PPC, Grosvenor Series 43.)

156

Happy children play by the lake in the late afternoon sun. (PPC, Valentine 69182, 1910.)

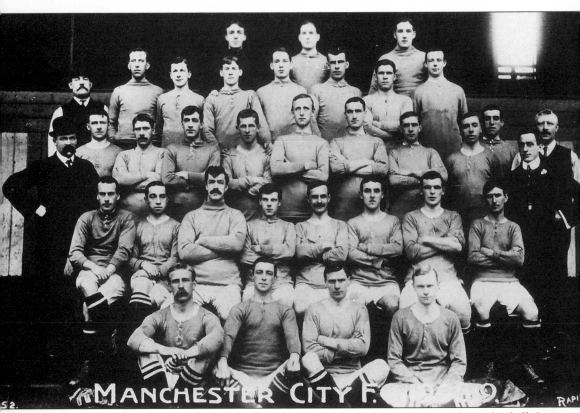

Manchester City Football Club, 1908-9. Manchester, it seems, was slow to take to football. In September 1880, a letter in the press, from "Old Association," of 23 Palatine St., Harpurhey, bemoaned the fact. "Sir, Coming from the south, I am surprised at the almost total absence in Manchester of the Association game. (*He seems to have been strangely unaware of the Newton Heath club which had been playing in a clay pit since 1878 and are regarded as the fore-runners of United.*) Doubtless many of your readers who are old Association men, or who would be football players, but who do not care for the rough hand-play and handling of the Rugby game, would be glad to assist in the formation of a club to play the Association rules. I have just started such a club in this district, and shall be glad of the co-operation of any of your readers." Someone out there must have been listening, for a West Gorton Club was started also that year, only to fail when the cricketers of Kirkmanshulme ejected them from their ground. After more disasters, the City club emerged in 1894. The Maine Road ground was opened on 25 August 1923. (PPC, Rapid Photo Co. 5152.)

St James Amateur Football Club, thought to be from Chorlton-on-Medlock, proudly posing with their trophies. (PPC, Reavy.)

Acknowledgements

My thanks are due to the many people who have helped me in editing this collection, either by filling in the gaps in my own collection with pictures of their own or from the archives for which they are responsible, in providing information, stimulating (or correcting) my memory or in various other ways. Among the works used for reference I should mention specially *The Stones of Manchester* by Cecil Stewart (Edward Arnold, 1956) and the local history books by Monty Dobkin (Neil Richardson, Radcliffe.)

Where possible I have given the source of the photographs in the text and I appreciate the permission granted for their use and for making them accessible by the following:

the Chief Executive of Manchester City Council, the City Engineer and Departmental staff,
the Directors of the Manchester Jewish Museum,
Philip Dunn, Registrar at the National Museum of Labour History,
the High Master and Governors of the Manchester Grammar School,
the Headmistress and Governors of the Manchester High School for Girls,
the National Tramway Museum, Crich, the *Manchester Evening News*,
the Co-operative Wholesale Society, J.Salmon Ltd., Sevenoaks
and Dennis Print & Publishing, Scarborough,
John Stewart and Stuart Marshall.
My apologies are due to any person whose name I have omitted because of failure to trace ownership.

I have had invaluable help and advice from the staff of the Central Library, Manchester and, among others, Ian Bailey, Monty Dobkin, Mary and Peter Rhodes, Rita Russell, Adrienne Wallman and George Waugh. David Buxton, Senior Editor of Chalford Publishing has been most helpful and supportive throughout. Finally I must thank my wife, Margaret, for her patience and encouragement over the past few months.

Key to Postcard Publishers

Publishing details of Picture Postcards (PPCs) are given beneath the illustrations. The following abbreviations have been used to identify publishers whose cards appear frequently:

AHC – A. Harold Clarke, Manchester
Grosvenor, Kingsway or WHS & S – W. H. Smith & Son
JLB – J. L. Brown, Manchester
Richter – C. Richter, London NW 6
Valentine – Valentine & Sons Ltd., Dundee
Ward – photographer, Oxford Road, Manchester